World War I

THE BEST ONE-HOUR HISTORY

Robert Freeman

The Best One-Hour History™

Kendall Lane Publishers, Palo Alto, CA

ISBN-13: 978-0-9892502-7-6

Contents

World War I Alliances

- Germany, Austria-Hungary, Italy = Triple Alliance
- England, France, Russia = Triple Entente
- All others

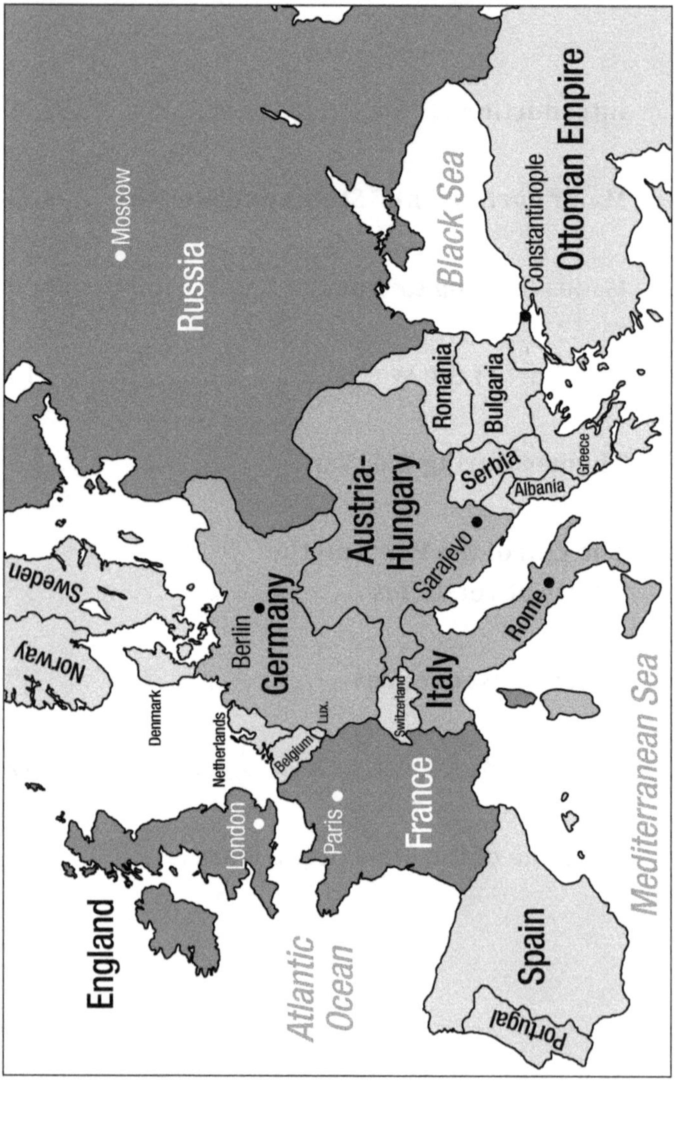
Russia
Moscow
Black Sea
Constantinople
Ottoman Empire
Romania
Bulgaria
Serbia
Albania
Greece
Austria-Hungary
Sarajevo
Rome
Italy
Sweden
Norway
Denmark
Berlin
Germany
Netherlands
Belgium
Lux.
Switzerland
France
Paris
England
London
Atlantic Ocean
Spain
Portugal
Mediterranean Sea

1 Introduction

In 1914, Europe blundered into one of the greatest cataclysms in history. It began a European civil war that would last for over four years, that would consume the entire continent and involve several other continents as well, and that would ultimately claim over 26 million casualties. It brought to bear the entire productive capacity of a modern technological civilization for the effective purpose of industrializing human slaughter.

Because of its sheer horror, the scale of its destruction, and its lasting impact, the causes of World War I have been studied for decades. At their root, they reflect what happens when a system designed for balance goes out of balance, when established powers become weak, when ambitious newcomers maneuver for more power, when all participants become schemers in an intricate web of alliances, and when all parties to a conflict have access to unending supplies of unimaginably destructive armaments.

This book examines each of the major participants in the War, including their strategic positions, national interests, and motivations for engaging in war. It looks at the underlying issues that virtually guaranteed a war, and then how the War actually started. It discusses themes during the War, how the War ended, and the Treaty of Versailles which settled the War. Finally, it considers some the War's major consequences and concludes with a final word and a timeline of the War's beginning.

The consequences of World War I were as dramatic as the devastation itself. They included: the extinction of four formerly great empires; the emergence of communism as a state-based system; the creation of 11 new countries; a proliferation of dictatorships; the end of European dominance in world affairs; and the elevation of the United States to the position of pre-eminent world power. Any one of these consequences would be momentous, at any place, or at any time. Their cumulative effect, as a result of a single event, is impossible to overstate. In fact, *the impact of World War I was so great, it is considered by many historians as the most significant event of the last thousand years.* This is that story.

2 Major Participants: Status and Motives

The major participants in World War I were Germany, France, Austria-Hungary, Russia, the Ottoman Empire, England, and the Balkan states. The United States joined the War in April 1918, six months before it was over. Since it was not involved in either the start of the War or the worst of its fighting, the U.S. was designated an "associate power" in the settlement negotiations of Versailles.

The central actor in the War, the country that prompted it, was Germany. Germany had become a unified country only in 1871 when a collection of Germanic states led by Otto von Bismarck of Prussia banded together to defeat France in the Franco-Prussian War. In that war, Germany's stunningly rapid victory humiliated France, which at the time was considered continental Europe's greatest power. This left France with both fear and enmity toward Germany. Fearful of French retaliation in the west and Russia looming to its east, Germany, in 1879, created a *Dual Alliance* with its fellow Germanic state, Austria-Hungary. It created another, more shallow alliance with Italy in 1882. This three-way union between Germany, Austria-Hungary and Italy was called the *Triple Alliance*. It was Germany's ambition to use the Alliance to gain influence in the crumbling Ottoman Empire to the south.

It was in France that most of the War's fighting occurred. Since the time of Charlemagne, France had been one of the leading powers of continental Europe. Its fortunes, however, had fallen in recent years. Napoleon's defeat in 1815 had been a huge blow to France's prestige, a setback from which it never fully recovered. And while it was fighting the French Revolution and the Napoleonic Wars, it fell far behind England in industrial power. Then, its recent loss to Germany in the Franco-Prussian War was another cause of bitterness and insecurity. Finally, France had fallen behind England in the race for colonies in the late 1800s. It sought to compensate for these losses and to balance rising German power, first, by allying itself with Russia, and then by patching up its historical differences with England. When England then made an alliance with Russia, the resulting *Triple Entente* (between France, England, and Russia) had the effect of encircling Germany and making it feel threatened.

Austria-Hungary is the state that fired first in the War. It was the last remaining descendant of the Holy Roman Empire, established in 800 A.D.

Since the 1300s, Austria had been one of the dominant monarchies in Europe. But it was now one of the most troubled players on the continent. It had a weak, agricultural economy and was ruled by a reactionary aristocratic elite. More important, it was deeply divided by ethnic and nationalistic strife. In 1911, there were 22 different parties in the Parliament. Many of these ethnic groups were pressing for national independence, similar to that achieved by Italians and Germans in the late 1800s. But Austria-Hungary believed that such recognition posed an existential threat to the integrity, even the survival of the Empire. As a result, Austria-Hungary felt constantly insecure. It had effectively made itself a vassal state of Germany. Austria-Hungary, Germany, and Italy made up the *Triple Alliance*.

Russia (after the Ottoman Empire) was the most backward of all the major players in Europe. Only in the late 1800s had it thrown off feudalism. It had very little industrialization. It was defeated by France and England in the Crimean War in the 1850s, and by Japan in the Russo-Japanese war in 1905. This latter loss was the first time a major European power had been defeated by a non-European power since the fall of Constantinople in 1453. It shook the Tsar's regime to its foundations. Because of its embrace of Orthodox Christianity, Russia believed it had legitimate claim to Constantinople, the "Rome" of the Eastern Orthodox Church. Russia also coveted the straits at Constantinople which connected the Mediterranean and Black Seas. Over the prior century Russia had repeatedly joined with other Slavic states in southeastern Europe to attack the Ottomans, almost pushing them out of Europe. Russia, France, and England made up the *Triple Entente.*

The land we know today as Turkey was the center of the Ottoman Empire. It was an Islamic theocratic empire whose ruler, the Sultan, was also the top religious figure, the Caliph. But the Ottomans had never modernized. Rather, they had fallen far behind European states in military strength, scientific achievement, material prosperity and political freedom for their people. As a result, it was called "the sick man of Europe." The Ottoman Empire controlled territories in the Middle East, north-Africa, and the Balkans in southeastern Europe. But by the last years of the 19th century it was being nibbled to death by stronger European powers. It sat astride the strategically vital straits between the Black Sea and the Mediterranean Sea, making it a constant target of Russian aggression. To fend off Russia, the Ottomans had made a pact with Germany, which wanted access to the oil fields in the southern Ottoman Empire in what is modern-day Iraq.

England, at the turn of the century was, by most accounts, the strongest country in the world. It controlled the largest global empire. It boasted the largest navy in the world, was the world's leader in international trade, and was the global leader in international finance. But its attentions to its empire over the prior century had left it isolated in Europe. It needed strong partners on the continent to counter the recent ascension of Germany. So, it formed alliances with its two arch-rivals. Its 1904 alliance with France, the *Entente Cordiale*, was designed to bolster France in its ability to stand up to Germany. Its 1907 accord with Russia, the *Anglo-Russian Accord*, put to rest hostilities between the two countries in Central Asia, hostilities which threatened England's colonial affairs in India and China. This *Triple Entente* between England, France, and Russia had the effect of encircling Germany and making it feel vulnerable.

The Balkans, named for the Balkan Mountains in southeastern Europe, are the place where World War I began. They had been controlled for centuries by the Ottoman Empire. But in 1821 Greece achieved independence from the Ottomans, setting off a later series of revolts which weakened the Empire. In the late 1800s, several Balkan countries fought wars with the Ottomans and gained independence. Serbia was one of the most fiercely nationalistic of these countries. It repeatedly challenged not just the Ottomans but Austria-Hungary as well, pushing for independence for the millions of Serbs who lived in the Austrian-Hungarian Empire. It was buttressed in both of these confrontations by its Slavic patron, Russia, which provocatively fanned the flames of Slavic nationalism in the Balkans.

The event that triggered World War I was the assassination in Sarajevo, Bosnia of Archduke Francis (Franz) Ferdinand, the "heir-apparent" to the Austrian-Hungarian throne. The date was June 28, 1914. Anti-imperial agitation had been carried out by Serbs living in Austria-Hungary and had been abetted by the Serbian government. As a result, Austria-Hungary believed that the Serbian government was either responsible or irresponsible in the death of Ferdinand. It demanded extraordinary concessions from Serbia, concessions that, if fully implemented, would have amounted to significant diminution of Serbia's national sovereignty. Russia declared that it would not stand idly by if its Slavic ally, Serbia, was subjected to such treatment. Russia had repeatedly made such declarations in the past, but had been forced to back down by the other powers of Europe. This time it would not back down.

3   Issues Leading to War

World War I was a conflict between European powers about who was going to gain control of the crumbling Ottoman Empire. The Empire had been repeatedly attacked over the prior century by England, Austria, Russia, France, and Italy and had been unable to effectively defend itself. It was one of the last contiguous areas on earth that could still be colonized in a period when it seemed that European powers (following the example of England) needed colonies to compete as global powers. After Germany became a unified nation in 1871, it began to look about for colonies that would be commensurate with its intended status as a world power. The Ottoman Empire, to the south of Austria-Hungary, was an irresistible temptation.

The British, however, were threatened by the growth of German power (see below) and were determined to check it. That is why, as mentioned above, it buried its long-standing rivalries with both Russia and France to form a united front against Germany. Compounding the attraction of the

Ottoman Empire for Germany (and the threat to England) was the fact that it contained some of the richest oil deposits in the world. The German engineer, Rudolph Diesel, had invented the diesel engine in the 1890s, helping Germany in its ascent to global economic power. An assured source of oil would only bolster that ascent. Control of the Ottoman Empire would give Germany control of a significant part of the world's known oil wealth. But such control would prove a dire threat to England which, in 1908, had converted its navy from coal to oil power. England's entire empire was managed by its vast global navy. So, when Germany moved in July 1914 to remove Serbia as the last obstacle to its alliance with the Ottomans, England felt it had no choice but to stop it.

Finally, there was Russia. For centuries Russia had challenged the Ottoman Empire for control of the straits at Constantinople where the Black Sea connects to the Mediterranean. In these contests, Russia had been largely successful, though many of its conquests had been rolled back by the other powers of Europe. But Constantinople and the straits were crucial to Russia, not just because of the religious reasons mentioned above, but because some 40% of Russia's exports transited through the straits on the way to markets around the world. Without assured access to the straits, Russia could not generate export earnings and its plans for industrial modernization could not be realized.

In other words, control of the straits was a life-and-death matter for Russia. That is why after the assassination of Franz Ferdinand in June 1914 Russia mobilized its army for war, even though it had no legal claims at issue in Serbia. It chose to use the opportunity created by Austria's intimidation of Serbia to check Germanic expansion into the Ottoman Empire. Beneath this fundamental European-wide imperial dynamic, there were many other issues leading to war.

The Tectonic Clash of Three Civilizations

The Balkan Mountains at the southeastern edge of Europe form a coming-together-point for three distinct civilizations: the Islamic/Turkish civilization of the Ottoman Empire; the Orthodox/Slavic civilization of the Russian Romanov Empire; and the Catholic/Germanic civilization of the Austrian-Hungarian Empire. For millennia this region had been the ground on which colossal cultural collisions had taken place. Dacia and Thrace (modern-day Romania and Bulgaria), were the northeastern limits of the Roman Empire. The Balkans are where the Chinese Mongols had been stopped in their westward expansion in 1241. And it is where Germany planned to pass through on its way to collecting the spoils of the collapsing Ottoman Empire. It is no surprise, therefore, that this should be the flash point for what would become at the time the greatest war in the history of the world.

The Rise of German Power

Germany's defeat of Austria in 1866 and France in 1871 upended Europe's balance of power. In the years after its victory, Germany's economy boomed. In coal, steel, machine tools, chemicals, electrical equipment and other industries, Germany was outpacing all of the other nations of Europe. Though England had led the world in the first Industrial Revolution—the one centered on textiles, iron, steam, and coal—it was Germany that led the Second Industrial Revolution—the one centering on chemicals, steel, internal combustion, and oil. The result was that whereas England's share of global wealth was 20 TIMES that of Germany in 1850, by 1913 Germany's share surpassed that of England by 50%. This was an astonishing, unprecedented reversal in relative economic power in such a short period of time. Left unchecked, it would lead to a reversal in military and state power as well. And in fact, Germany had built the largest and most modern army in Europe and in the late 1890s began an aggressive program of military shipbuilding aimed at challenging England's supremacy of the world's oceans.

Balkan Nationalism

The Balkan people were ethnic Slavs who had been ruled for centuries as part of the Ottoman Empire. But they had a burning desire for autonomy, fueled by the nationalism that had swept Europe after the French Revolution. In 1878, Russia and several Balkan states fought the Ottoman Empire and drove it all the way to Constantinople. Though they defeated the Ottomans on the battlefield, many of their gains were reversed by the Great Powers which sought to maintain a "balance of power" in Europe. The result was a deep animosity, especially toward Austria-Hungary which appeared to have unfairly gained at their expense. This resentment deepened in 1908 when Austria-Hungary annexed Bosnia and Herzegovina, depriving Serbia of its planned take-over of the region. Finally, in 1913, although Serbia was on the winning side of the Second Balkan War it was denied access to the Adriatic Sea when Austria-Hungary helped create the state of Albania. The result of all these events was to make the Serbs implacable enemies of Austria-Hungary.

Austrian-Hungarian Weakness

By the late 1800s Austria-Hungary was a paralyzed giant. It had lost provinces to Italian unification in 1860. It had lost a war with Prussia (Germany) in 1866. In 1867, Austria was forced to give semi-autonomy to Hungary following a revolt. This left the new empire divided between two rulers. Worse, Hungary mistreated the Slavs within its territory, making enemies of the very people Austria most needed to placate. In response, the Slavic states to the south of Austria-Hungary, especially Serbia, were constantly stoking resentment among the Slavs who lived within the Empire. The Empire was already riven by deep ethnic divisions. Within Austria-Hungary there lived more than a dozen different peoples—Germans, Italians, Poles, Czechs, Hungarians, Slavs, Bulgarians, Armenians, Serbs, Croats, Rumanians, Jews, Gypsies, and more. This hodge-podge of ethnicities made it difficult to rule the Empire and virtually impossible to reach accommodation with its secessionist Slav population in the south.

The Collapsing Ottoman Empire

Weakness in the Ottoman Empire invited aggression from the stronger states of Europe. As mentioned above, the Ottomans lost control of Bulgaria, Romania, Montenegro, and Serbia in the Russo-Turkish War of 1878. It lost control of Egypt in 1882. It lost administrative control of Bosnia-Herzegovina in the same conflict and complete control when Austria-Hungary moved to annex Bosnia-Herzegovina in 1908. It surrendered the north-African territories of Algeria, Tunisia, and Morocco to France in the late 1800s. In 1911, it lost its northern-African state of Libya to the naked aggression of Italy. In the First Balkan war, the Balkan League drove the Ottomans to the edge of the European continent. In all these events, the Ottomans proved impotent in resisting aggression. Germany, late to the imperial game, was among those nations most anxious to gain Ottoman territory, but it would have to pass to the south through its ally, Austria-Hungary, and the impediment of Serbia to be able to do this.

Russian Ambitions in the Balkans

For centuries, Russia had had ambitions to "reclaim" Constantinople. While it had defeated the Ottomans in the Russo-Turkish War, it was humiliated when some of those gains were reversed by the other powers of Europe in the Treaty of Berlin. In 1908, Russia made a secret agreement with Austria-Hungary that Russia would take the straits at Constantinople and Austria-Hungary would annex Bosnia-Herzegovina. Austria-Hungary got its gains but Russia was denied hers—once again by the other powers of Europe. Finally, in 1912, the Balkan League, acting under Russian patronage, attacked the Ottomans and all but drove them out of Europe. And once again, other European powers intervened to deny Russia and its Balkan client states what they viewed as their rightful gains. In the Second Balkan War, in 1913, Bulgaria was defeated, dealing a serious blow to the Russo-Bulgarian alliance. This left Russia with only Serbia as a reliable Balkan ally. Its prestige as a patron to the smaller Slavic Balkan states thus became a critical issue, making it impossible to back down in the next confrontation, in 1914.

German Aggressiveness in Pushing Austria-Hungary to War

Germany used Austria-Hungary as its proxy to provoke a war against Serbia for access to territory in the Middle East. This occurred for two reasons. First, by 1907, Germany's foes had united in the *Triple*

Entente to limit German power. Austria-Hungary, its kindred German state to the south, was the only ally it could count on. Second, Germany believed that war with France and Russia was inevitable. It felt it should strike while it still had the upper hand and before the other countries could catch up with its recently accelerated weapons-building program. Germany repeatedly pushed Austria-Hungary to control the "upstart" countries in the Balkans to the south. After the assassination of Archduke Francis Ferdinand in June, 1914, Germany issued a "blank check" to Austria-Hungary, promising that it would back the monarchy in neutralizing Serbian resistance. These assurances prompted Austria-Hungary to provoke war with Serbia, as they were meant to do, leading Russia to come to the defense of its smaller Slavic neighbor.

The Domino Effect of Entangling Alliances

Germany had formed the *Dual Alliance* with Austria-Hungary in 1879. Italy joined in 1882 making it the *Triple Alliance*. Similarly, in 1894, France formed an alliance with Russia, the Franco-Russian Alliance. Then, in 1904, France buried historical rivalries and formed an alliance with England, the *Entente Cordiale*. Finally, England created an alliance with Russia in 1907, the *Anglo-Russian Accord*. This completed the *Triple Entente* which set itself off against the *Triple Alliance*. The domino effect of these entangling alliances came into play once hostilities began. Austria-Hungary declared war on Serbia on July

28, 1914. As an ally and patron of Serbia, Russia mobilized its army on July 30th. Germany took this to be a threat to its ally, Austria-Hungary, and declared war on Russia on August 1st. Certain that France would come to the aid of its ally, Russia, Germany declared war on France two days later, August 3rd. England responded to the attack on her ally, France, by declaring war on Germany on August 4th. Within seven days, a minor border skirmish in a remote region of Europe had dragged all of the major powers into war.

Military Preparations Making War Inevitable

By 1907, all of the major countries of Europe had begun preparing for war. The German plan dictated a lightning strike to defeat France in the west. Once completed, Germany would pivot to the east where it would subdue Russia. This was the Schlieffen Plan, named for its author, Count Alfred von Schlieffen, head of the German General Staff. For its part, France had Plan XVII which ordered an offensive thrust into Alsace and Lorraine to force the Germans into a defensive position. Plan XVII was developed in conjunction with the Russians who had promised to begin offensive action against Germany within 50 days of any attack. These plans assumed massive importance as tensions mounted in the summer of 1914. The belief of the generals was that inaction in the face of mobilization by an enemy would produce assured defeat—a "use them or lose them" mentality which created its own inescapable momentum. Once the real prospect of hostilities emerged, all parties gave significant control—or lost significant control—of their states' actions to their militaries. The march to war then took on a life of its own. As each side mobilized, the other side *had* to escalate still further to avoid losing its military assets to a rapid first strike by the enemy. This dynamic assuredly accelerated the race to war.

4   The Start of the War

As the above sections made clear, tensions leading up to the start of the War had been building for decades. At their heart, they concerned shifting patterns of power in a political system that was incapable of making meaningful adjustments to such changes. The event that actually set fire to this "keg of gunpowder," therefore, was remarkably simple and, if not innocent, at least unforeseen.

The heir-apparent to the Austrian throne, Archduke Francis Ferdinand, was visiting Sarajevo in Bosnia, the southernmost region of the Empire. On June 28th, 1914, he was assassinated in his car by a 19 year-old Serbian anarchist, Gavrilo Princip. Austria-Hungary accused the government of Serbia of being complicit in the murder. Serbia was probably not directly involved, though it had tolerated anti-Imperial nationalism that made the assassination much more likely. In consequence, Austria-Hungary issued an "Ultimatum" demanding Serbian concessions. The concessions were extremely onerous. Some of them, if accepted, would have resulted in losses of Serbian political autonomy.

Despite the extreme nature of the Ultimatum, Serbia replied in a conciliatory manner, conceding to virtually all of the demands. But it rejected three of the demands, requesting clarification and negotiation. Austria-Hungary rejected Serbia's conciliatory response. This was expected as the Ultimatum was, in fact, crafted so as to be intolerable to Serbia, ensuring its rejection. On July 28th, three days after the rejection, Austria-Hungary declared war on Serbia and began shelling its capital, Belgrade.

It is significant that on July 5th—*after* the murder but *before* the issuance of the Ultimatum—Germany issued its notorious "Blank Check" to Austria-Hungary. The Blank Check assured Austria-Hungary that Germany would support it in any confrontation with either Serbia or, should it decide to intervene, Russia. With the Blank Check in hand, Austria-Hungary acted in a more bellicose manner than it would have without such backing. Russian diplomats recognized this immediately and understood that it was really Germany who was behind the Ultimatum and that they *wanted* it to be rejected. The Blank Check is considered by most historians the "smoking gun" of Germany's instigation of the War, albeit through its proxy, Austria-Hungary.

Once Austria-Hungary rejected Serbia's reply to its Ultimatum, the sequence of events leading to war became more or less automatic—the domino effect noted above. Russia realized that if it did not defend its ally, Serbia, its Balkan strategy and its standing as a reliable power would be in shambles. So, it mobilized its army, confronting both Austria-Hungary and Germany with a "use them or lose them" situation concerning their forces. Germany could not leave its troops idle in the face of such a threat and so declared war on Russia. Then, in carrying out the Schlieffen Plan, it declared war on France and invaded Belgium on its way to Paris. England, committed to come to the aid of its ally, Russia, declared war on Germany under the pretext that Germany had violated Belgian neutrality. France declared war on Germany as well. The dominoes had fallen with stunning rapidity. Within a month of the assassination, all of Europe was at war.

The problem for Germany was that it now faced a two-front war. The *Triple Entente* meant that Germany was surrounded and would have to fight both France in the west, and Russia in the east. Its strategy for dealing with this challenge was to reduce the problem to a sequence of two rapid one-front wars. It would carry out a lightning strike on France in the west, taking it out of the war, then pivot to the east to deal with Russia. This was the Schlieffen Plan, mentioned above.

The premise of the plan was that France would be the more agile of the two foes, but could be quickly defeated by an end run of its defenses in a sweeping arc through Belgium, along the English Channel, and around the back side of Paris. It was assumed that Russia would be slower to mobilize than France, and that with France out of the War, German troops could be shipped via railway across the continent to deal with Russia in the east. As is so often the case with military planning before war, both of these assumptions failed once war began.

Though he wrote the plan that bore his name, it was not Schlieffen who carried it out. He died in 1913. His successor, Helmuth von Moltke, was less daring than Schlieffen and held back forces that Schlieffen had insisted were necessary to complete the encirclement of Paris. Also, the Russians mobilized their army more quickly than the Schlieffen Plan had assumed they would, exposing Germany to invasion from the east. In response, Moltke removed still more troops from the western front in order to bolster the line in the east.

The result was that the German army was stretched too thin to carry out its intended encirclement of Paris. Instead, it shrunk the arc, turning inward before reaching the city, and exposing its right flank to the French army. The French attacked the Germans at the Marne River, 14 miles outside of Paris, handing the Germans their first and decisive defeat. The Germans fell back 35 miles to the Lower Aisne River where they dug trenches as defensive fortifications.

This doomed the Germans' hopes of a quick victory over the French and, therefore, their entire strategy for winning the War. Barely a month after the War had started, Moltke suffered a nervous breakdown, telling the Kaiser, "Your majesty, we have lost the War." He was correct. He was relieved of duty but the damage was done. The Germans would remain in their trenches until 1918, defining one of the most prominent themes of World War I: trench warfare.

Germany and Austria-Hungary would be joined by Bulgaria and the Ottoman Empire as the "Central Powers." France, Russia and England were called the "Allies." Italy failed to join Germany and Austria-Hungary as was committed by its membership in the *Triple Alliance*. It initially declared neutrality, but in 1915 joined the Allies against its former treaty signatories. Nobody suspected it at the time, but the War would prove the bloodiest conflict in the history of the world up to that time.

5 Themes During the War

Stalemate

Most of the European wars of the prior century had been brisk affairs—over in a matter of weeks. Few people believed at the War's outset, therefore, that it could possibly go on for four unremitting years. The British press even announced at the War's beginning that "the boys will be home for Christmas." It was a grievously failed belief. The reason is that the War became stalemated within a few weeks of its beginning, a result of the trench warfare mentioned above, and could not be undone.

A line of trenches was dug stretching 400 miles from Switzerland in the east to the English Channel in the west. These were guarded by barbed wire and concrete "pillboxes" housing machine gunners and backed by long-range artillery. Such defensive fighting characterized most of the War on the Western front. The stalemate it produced is one of the reasons the war was so costly and difficult to end.

For example, in the five months of fighting at the Battle of the Somme River in France, 1.2 million lives were lost while the line of battle was advanced only seven miles. Stalemate lasting for years thus became one of the most distinctive characteristics of World War I.

New Industrial Technologies

The War proved the staging ground for many new and revolutionary technologies. Consider, for example, that only a century before, Napoleon's troops took as long to march from Paris to Italy as had Caesar's two thousand years before. In World War I, however, a network of continental-wide railroads allowed the movement of troops and supplies at more than 10 times Napoleon's speed. Telegraph systems also accelerated the pace of decision-making from far behind front lines. These two technologies did much to change the face of warfare in the twentieth century. It was in the arena of armaments, however, that the greatest revolution had taken place.

World War I saw the first widespread use of machine guns, hand grenades, airplanes, submarines, tanks, trench warfare, flame-throwers, and chemical gasses. These technologies changed not just the pace of war but the very nature of war itself, making it incalculably more costly, deadly, impersonal, and inhuman. Compounding the effects of the weapons, World War I was the first war where the industrial plants of all of the combatants were pressed into continuous service in support of the seemingly unending fighting. This is one of the reasons the War proved so unexpectedly destructive: most past wars were fought until the ammunition ran out. This war offered generals on both sides essentially unending supplies of the most destructive armaments ever devised.

Massive Slaughter

Battlefield stalemate and new industrial technologies were combined with the sheer stupidity of military commanders to produce casualties on a scale never before known. The battle for Verdun in France in 1916 produced 970,000 casualties, the most of any single battle in the history of the world up until that time. But later in the same year, at the Somme River to the west, casualties surpassed 1.2 million. In a single hour of the worst fighting at the Somme, more than 30,000 soldiers were killed. Similar carnage at Ypres, Passchendaele, and other battles have made World War I a byword for senseless, unstoppable slaughter.

By the end of the War, military deaths on both sides reached 10 million. Civilian deaths reached 6 million, and civilian and military wounded exceeded 10 million—a total of 26 million dead and wounded. Such scale of death and destruction dwarfed by a factor of ten the losses in any war, ever. The sheer scale of the killing and the fact that so much of it was mechanized and impersonal, combined with the inability of anybody to stop it, would prove among the most perplexing of all the mysteries of the War. It would haunt Europe for decades to come, inflicting great trauma on the European psyche.

War in the Middle East

The main fighting of the War took place along the Western Front, in France. But once it bogged down there, the Allies, led by Britain, looked for another opening through which to attack. The most logical avenue was through the Ottoman Empire at the eastern end of the Mediterranean. The Ottomans were allied with Germany in the War and were potentially unstable. If Britain could defeat or destabilize them, it could attack the Central Powers from the south, through the Balkans, forcing Germany to divert resources from the Western Front. Britain tried several different strategies to achieve this. The first was an attack on the Mediterranean mouth of the straits, at a point called Gallipoli. It was a horrific failure, claiming the lives of over 250,000 Allied soldiers and a similar number of Ottoman defenders.

The second effort was an attempt to promote rebellion by the ethnic Arabs against their rulers, the Ottoman Turks. To foster this rebellion, the British promised in a series of communiques called the *McMahon Letters* that they would support Arab calls for national independence after the

War. At the same time, the British told the Jews in the *Balfour Declaration* that Britain would support the establishment of a "homeland" for the Jews in Palestine. Finally, the British made deals with the French in the *Sykes-Picot Accord* to divide up the Middle East between themselves following victory. Obviously, all of these conflicting commitments could not be fulfilled at the same time. As victors in the War, the British and French carried out the *Sykes-Picot Accord*, dismembering the Ottoman Empire and awarding the spoils to themselves. They did not keep their promises to either the Arabs or the Jews. The turmoil that still roils the Middle East today owes much of its origin to the conflict, promises, and settlement of World War I.

The Russian Revolution

Russia had long been the most backward country in Europe. Its political and economic systems were closer to those of the Middle Ages than they were to a modern European state. It had only finally abolished serfdom in the 1880s. When, in 1905, Japan defeated Russia in the far east, Russia suffered an uprising where rebels demanded political reform. The Tsar promised changes but quickly backed out of actually implementing anything. When the War with Germany began, Russia proved unable to withstand the concerted attack by German's ultra-modern army. Military losses mounted and economic breakdown ensued. The army began to mutiny and confidence in the government collapsed. By early 1917, the country fell into civil war. In March of 1917, in the face of erupting rebellion, the Tsar abdicated.

By October, a small group of tightly organized radicals called Bolsheviks seized control of the government. The Bolsheviks were led by Vladimir Lenin whose political philosophy was based on the works of Karl Marx. They were communists. Their motto, "Bread, Land, Peace" was one of the most effective marketing slogans of all time. Bread appealed to the urban workers, Land to the peasants, and Peace to the soldiers. While the Revolution was still young, a coalition of military forces from the United States, Britain, France, and Japan invaded Russia to try to undo the Revolution. This "White Counter-Revolution" was defeated but deeply poisoned future relations between Russia and the West. By the early 1920s, Lenin stabilized the country and installed the world's first communist government. The conflict between communism and capitalism, led by Russia on the one hand and the United States on the other, became the dominant global conflict of the second half of the twentieth century—The Cold War.

State Propaganda

States have propagandized their people since Pericles rallied the Athenians against the Spartans in the Peloponnesian Wars in the fifth century B.C. But it was in World War I that modern, industrial-scale propaganda was really born. Within days of the start of the War, the British cut the Germans' transatlantic telegraph cable to the U.S., ensuring that the Americans would receive only the British view of the war. The British government undertook a massive campaign to propagandize the U.S. with the aim of getting it into the War. It set up special "news" bureaus that distributed false stories of "atrocities" by the Germans. It cultivated American reporters with carefully choreographed tours behind the front lines. It sent hundreds of thousands of "information packages" to the roster of *Who's Who in America.* It worked. Though Woodrow Wilson ran in 1916 on the slogan "He kept us out of war," immediately after the election U.S. policy shifted to intervention. The problem was how to turn the American people around.

In the U.S. a Committee of Public Information (CPI) was set up and began blanketing the nation with propaganda urging the country to war. Tens of thousands of men were trained to speak in favor of the War and gave over 750,000 pro-war speeches to audiences around the country. Newspapers and magazines were given pro-war articles to run, while millions of pro-war pamphlets and posters were printed and distributed. Public libraries and schools were used as dissemination points of pro-war propaganda. The CPI produced a weekly pro-war newsreel, *The Official War Review,* that was shown in thousands of theaters every week. The

CPI harassed, censored, and stigmatized socialists, pacifists, and anti-war groups, accusing them of being un-American, even traitorous. The campaign joined government and private media in the most expansive campaign of public persuasion ever conceived. It set the model that still operates today for how to engineer public support for wars.

The U.S. Breaks the Stalemate

The U.S. had remained neutral throughout the early stages of the War. But as the War progressed, and especially after Russia dropped out following the Russian Revolution, it became clear that without American assistance the Allies might lose. American banks, which had financed the Allies during the War, stood to lose their substantial investments. Also, a German campaign of submarine warfare against Allied shipping had antagonized the American public when it sank the merchant ship *Lusitania* with Americans onboard. In April, 1917, the U.S. declared war against Germany.

Though it landed a small contingent of troops in Europe in June 1917, it wasn't until April 1918 that the U.S. landed 2 million soldiers and backed them up with fresh weapons and supplies. This broke the back of the German military which by then was exhausted, depleted, and demoralized from four years of unending combat. By July of 1918, the Germans were in full retreat and by November had surrendered. Without the American intervention, it is impossible to say how long the War would have continued or even who might have won. Because of its late entrance, the U.S. was not considered an "Allied" power in the post-War settlement talks but was named an "Associate" power, facilitating the War's end.

6 The End of the War and the Treaty of Versailles

In September 1918 Bulgaria surrendered, the first of the Central Powers to do so. In October, the Ottomans did so as well. In early November, Austria-Hungary surrendered. And on November 11, 1918, "at the eleventh hour of the eleventh day of the eleventh month," all was quiet on the western front. The Allies had won. The final settlement of the War, however, would take more than two years and multiple treaties to work out.

At issue were such concerns as: assigning guilt for the war; ensuring security against future acts of aggression; imposing reparations for damages done; and reconfiguring the political map of Europe to reflect the new realities of national power and ethnic identities. These challenges would prove too big for the diplomats and national leaders who created the settlement.

As the defeated party, Germany had to accept the terms dictated by the victors in the Treaty of Versailles. Vengeance, primarily from France, drove the Allied position. German territory, with many millions of German inhabitants, was taken away and added to the newly created state of Poland. A region in southeastern Germany, the Sudetenland, with over 5 million German-speaking inhabitants, was included in the newly created country of Czechoslovakia. Alsace and Lorraine, the territories Germany had taken from France in 1870, were returned to France together with a powerful coal-producing region, the Saar. Germany and Austria were forbidden to ever unify. German colonies in Africa were divided between England and France while German colonies in Asia were partitioned between England and Japan.

This "carving up" of Germany weakened the German economy, as it was intended to do, and bred deep resentment among the German people. Reuniting these dispersed German people would become one of the main ambitions and central appeals of Adolph Hitler in the 1920s and 1930s. Hitler carried out his promise to reunite the German people, annexing Austria (this was the backdrop of the movie, *The Sound of Music*), the Sudetenland, the rest of Czechoslovakia, and ultimately invading Poland. It was one of the direct causes of World War II.

Perhaps most damaging was the assignment of reparations. France insisted that Germany make huge payments, both as a penalty for having started the War and for the damage that had been inflicted during the War. (The fighting on the Western Front had almost all taken place in France.) France's real intent was to "bleed Germany white" in the expectation that such impositions would prevent Germany from rebuilding its military and ever regaining the continental power it had amassed.

These reparations included billions of marks (dollars), millions of tons of ships, thousands of railroad cars and engines, millions of tons of coal and iron, millions of tons of kerosene, benzene, and other industrial chemicals, huge amounts of agricultural commodities and livestock, and the disgorgement of all of Germany's colonies in Africa and Asia. The economist John Maynard Keynes who represented the British Treasury at the conference, quit the Versailles Conference in disgust and wrote a prophetic book about the settlement, *The Economic Consequences of the Peace.* In it, he predicted that the settlement of Versailles would lead within another generation to another European-wide war. History would prove him right.

The combined effect of all these impositions was to make it impossible for Germany to rebuild her economy in the years following the War. This led, ultimately, to the collapse of the German economy in the early 1920s and the destruction of its middle class through a horrific inflation of the money supply. It would give a foothold to political extremism in the form of Adolph Hitler, who capitalized on the economic collapse and on German resentment of its treatment at Versailles to build up his Nazi party.

The acrimony surrounding the Versailles negotiations proved so venomous that Americans were repulsed. The U.S. Senate reacted by rejecting Woodrow Wilson's proposal for a League of Nations intended to maintain world peace. Instead, the U.S. turned inward in the years following the end of the War and practiced two decades of relative isolation. This contributed to the collapse of the international financial system in the late 1920s and the international political system in the 1930s. As such, it, too, contributed to the eventual return to World War in 1939.

7   Major Consequences

All wars have consequences. Major wars have major consequences. But no war in the history of the world has had consequences at once so many, so momentous, so far-reaching, and so long lasting as did World War I. It is the cumulative effect of these consequences—their number, their scale, their scope, and their duration—that makes World War I one of the most significant events of the last thousand years.

Destruction of Four Great Empires

Four great empires perished in World War I. They were: 1) the Austrian-Hungarian Empire which was the direct descendant of the Holy Roman Empire and (the Austrian portion of which) had ruled much of Europe since the early 1300s. It was dismembered into various countries in central and eastern Europe; 2) the Romanov Empire of the Tsars which had ruled Russia for over 400 years. It was replaced by the communist government of the Bolsheviks which lasted until 1991; 3) the Ottoman Empire which had ruled much of southwestern Asia and southeastern Europe for over 500 years. It was carved up into six separate nations with five of them put under the control of England and France; and 4) the German (Hohenzollern) Empire which had assumed power in 1648 at the end of the Thirty Years War. It was dramatically reduced in size and its government replaced with the Weimar Republic. Never before in the history of the world had so many massive empires expired together in a single event.

Emergence of New States

Eleven new countries emerged out of the settlement that followed World War I. Six of these countries were created to build a "buffer" to separate communist Russia from capitalist Europe, the infamous "Cordon Sanitaire" or sanitary corridor. They also addressed the demand for self-determination by some 40 million dislocated people. These newly-created countries included (in Europe) Latvia, Estonia, Lithuania, Poland, Czechoslovakia, and Yugoslavia. In the Middle East, five additional new countries were created by carving up the defeated Ottoman Empire. These new countries, Palestine, Jordan, Syria, Lebanon and Iraq, were called "mandates" under the newly organized League of Nations. In fact, they were quasi-colonies of France and England.

Many of these areas remain unstable even today. Note, for example, that six major wars have occurred since 1948 between the Jews and

Arabs in the former Ottoman territory that was called Palestine. In the early 1990s the United States fought Iraq in the Persian Gulf War and in 2003 invaded Iraq. Lebanon has been a source of repeated instability since its founding in 1920. Note, too, that Yugoslavia was the location of two wars in the 1990s. Syria, a secular state, is under attack today (2013) by fundamentalist rebels supported by the U.S., France, and England.

Emergence of Communism as a State-Based System

The Russian Revolution gave birth to the world's first communist regime. At first it was unstable but it quickly righted itself and began a stunning economic transformation, vastly outperforming the nations of the Western world during the capitalist collapse of the Great Depression. In the first twenty years of its existence, however, the communist government caused the deaths of more than 40 million of its own citizens through political purges and deportation to the gulags (prison camps) of Siberia. This was more than three times the number of deaths in the whole of World War I itself. After World War II, Russia expanded its empire to include the countries of Eastern Europe, those that had been created as "buffers" for the West in the aftermath of World War I. From 1946 until its collapse in 1991, the Soviet Union would challenge the U.S. for supremacy in global affairs in the Cold War.

Rise of Dictatorships

The nineteenth century had been one of widespread political liberalization in Europe. Many of its countries had either overturned the rule of kings or had subordinated their monarchies to the practice of constitutionalism. But World War I so decimated the political structure of Europe that the prior century of political progress was quickly reversed. Eighteen countries in Europe became dictatorships in the aftermath of World War I. Many were the newly created countries, but not all of them. They included Russia, Hungary, Italy, Germany, Yugoslavia, Greece, Poland, and Spain. Taken together, this represented the most rapid and widespread regression of political progress in history. It presaged the descent of the whole of eastern Europe into communist dictatorship at the end of World War II.

Death of the European Enchantment

For five centuries—since the beginning of the Renaissance around 1400—Europe had considered itself the most advanced civilization on earth. With the Scientific Revolution, it had (it believed) vanquished superstition and elevated Reason to the role of decision-making in human affairs. With the Enlightenment it had invented Progress—the unending perfection of human society and even human beings by humans themselves. Its Industrial Revolution produced the most prodigiously productive civilization in the history of the world.

With its opera and ballet, painting and architecture, literature and philosophy, it had reached the apex of cultural achievement—the automatic production of Beauty and Knowledge as a routine by-product of human consciousness. All of that was blown to smithereens in World War I.

How could it be that civilized men could not avoid such a debacle? How could any civilization that sponsored such horrific, mass-scale, unending, mechanized butchery even consider itself civilized? What was wrong with European civilization that it would find its deepest urges to be so essentially destructive, in fact, suicidal, and on such a massive, collective scale? Europe's confidence in its philosophical underpinnings, even its very sanity, was deeply shaken. The recurrence of an even greater war only twenty years later on would only add fuel to the fire of doubt that had destroyed Europe's (and the rest of the world's) certainty of its inherent superiority.

Rise of the U.S. to Preeminent World Power

Because the War had been fought on the European continent, the U.S. emerged from it almost completely unscathed. Its people, its cities, its farms and factories were not only intact, they were actually in far better condition than when the War had begun, for they had supplied the European Allies with all that they needed to fight the War. American cities bustled, its factories boomed, and American farms had industrialized to help her Allies win the War. When the War was over and the smoke subsided, America found itself with the largest, most modern, and most productive economy in the world, by far. And it was to the U.S. that Europe had to turn to rebuild itself in the following decades.

Additionally, loans from America had made it possible for the Allies to fight and win the War. The U.S. would be rewarded with repayments from European governments for decades to come. Finally, the American president, Woodrow Wilson, offered a vision of a new world order based on his famous Fourteen Points. They included such lofty ideals as self-determination for all peoples, open treaties, and an outline for a League of Nations. For all these reasons, then, the U.S. emerged as not only the strongest economic and military power in the world but as the most prestigious, respected, and admired country as well. World War I was the once-in-the-history-of-the-world turning point at which the center of world power shifted from Europe to the United States.

The Cause of World War II

The combination of the loss of the War, the German humiliation from the Versailles settlement, and the collapse of the German economy in the inflation of the early 1920s led to titanic upheaval in German politics. Conservative forces conspired to undermine the Weimar Republic, the liberal government that was put in place after the War. Despite the fact that it was the conservatives who had started, prosecuted, and lost the War, they accused liberals, republicans, and Jews of having sold out the country, "stabbed it in the back," causing Germany to lose the War. The charges were false but were given credence by the fact that there was never a formal surrender document signed by Germany to end the War.

Additionally, the newly communist government of Russia repudiated the debts of its Tzarist predecessors. This caused a cascading series of financial defaults throughout Europe that finally culminated in the Great Depression of the 1930s. During the Depression, the German economy, like those of the rest of the Western world, collapsed. Traditional political parties were discredited and the National Socialist Party (Nazis), led by Adolph Hitler, seized power. Hitler promised the German people that he would erase the humiliation of the defeat in World War I, reunite the German people, and restore Germany to its rightful (he claimed superior) place in the world. The aggression that flowed from this led directly to World War II.

8 Final Word

World War I is an unequaled case study in ambition, uncertainty, intrigue, fear, arrogance, resentment, aggression, reprisal, hostility, betrayal, intimidation, miscalculation—in other words, a geopolitical soap-opera of truly Olympian proportions. Only it was not a myth. It was a reality unlike anything the world had ever seen before, carried out between modern (and semi-modern) nations competing for wealth, power, prestige, territory, and national glory.

The War reorganized the contours of global power more quickly and to greater effect than any event in the history of the world. Its flawed settlement led to enduring conflicts in Eastern Europe and the Middle East, conflicts that are still being played out today. It began the dissolution of European colonial empires that had been built up over the prior 400 years. World War II can be considered simply the delayed conclusion to the deeper European conflict that was first expressed in World War I but that remained unresolved in its deeply flawed settlement.

And the emergence of a communist-oriented state system in Russia became the central drama in the 45-year long Cold War that began immediately after World War II.

For these reasons, the importance of the Great War looms even larger than its immediate effect would suggest. Indeed, some of its effects would not even become apparent until after the end of World War II, twenty-five years later. The "War to End All Wars" as it was called at the time proved only a dress rehearsal to an even greater conflagration that would begin in 1939. That Second World War in only 20 years would prove five times as deadly as the first and wrap even more of the globe into its deadly embrace. It would drive the final nail into the coffin of European global superiority, passing that mantle, at least for a while, to the United States.

9 Timeline of the Start of the War

1871   The modern German state is created in the aftermath of the Franco-Prussian War.

1878   Bulgaria (with Russian help) revolts from the Ottoman Empire. The Ottomans lose Rumania, Montenegro and Serbia as well. Control of Bosnia and Herzegovina goes to Austria-Hungary. The Ottomans are virtually driven out of Europe. Russian ambition for Balkan gain is frustrated by European Powers.

1879   Austria-Hungary and Germany form *Dual Alliance* guaranteeing mutual defense if either is attacked by Russia.

1882   Italy joins Austria-Hungary and Germany to form *Triple Alliance*. High point of German diplomacy and strategic position in Europe.

1894   French treaty with Russia, surrounding Germany, forcing Germany to prepare to fight a two-front war. Germany begins preparation of Schlieffen Plan.

1904   *Entente Cordiale* between traditional enemies, France and England.

1905   Russia is defeated in Russo-Japanese War. Greatly weakened as a European power, Russia must seek allies to maintain European position.

1907   *Anglo-Russian Accord* between England and Russia, burying mutual hostility. *Triple Entente*, the alliance of England, France and Russia, is now complete, finalizing German encirclement.

1912   First Balkan War. Newly formed Balkan League—Greece, Montenegro, Bulgaria and Serbia—defeats Ottomans (with the help of Russia). Aggressors' gains undone by the Great Powers. Russia humiliated. Slav states frustrated.

1913   Second Balkan War. Unhappy with its gains from the first Balkan War, Bulgaria attacks Serbia but loses. At Austrian-Hungarian urging, Albania is created to deny Serbia access to Adriatic Sea. Austria-Hungary now faces an angry, united pan-Slavic Balkan contingent of Serbia, Romania, Greece and Montenegro.

1914	June 28.	Serbian anarchist Gavrilo Princip assassinates Archduke Francis Ferdinand, heir-apparent to the Austrian throne.
	July 5.	Germany issues Blank Check to Austria-Hungary.
	July 23.	Austria-Hungary issues Ultimatum to Serbia.
	July 25.	Serbia conciliates but Austria-Hungary rejects its response.
	July 28.	Austria-Hungary declares war on Serbia.
	July 30.	Russia announces mobilization of its army in preparation for war.
	August 1.	Germany declares war on Russia. Schlieffen Plan is set in motion.
	August 2.	Germany invades Luxembourg.
	August 3.	Germany declares war on France, invades Belgium.

August 4. England declares war on Germany.

August 5. Montenegro declares war on Austria-Hungary.

August 6. Austria-Hungary declares war on Russia.

Serbia declares war on Germany.

The entire European continent is at war.

If you enjoyed this book, please look for all of the titles in *The Best One-Hour History* series.

- Ancient Greece
- Rome
- The Middle Ages
- The Renaissance
- The Protestant Reformation
- European Wars of Religion
- The English Civil Wars
- The Scientific Revolution
- The Enlightenment
- The American Revolution
- The French Revolution
- The Industrial Revolution
- Europe in the 1800s
- The American Civil War
- European Imperialism
- World War I
- The Interwar Years
- World War II
- The Cold War
- The Vietnam War

To learn more about each title and its expected publication date, visit: *http://onehourhistory.com*

If you could change the world for a dollar, would you?

Well, you CAN. *Now*, WILL you?

One Dollar For Life™ helps American students build schools in the developing world, for a dollar. *We can help you build one, too!*

Since 2007, we've built 15 schools and 23 infrastructure projects in countries like Nepal, Haiti, Nicaragua, Kenya, Malawi, and South Africa.

Imagine if you and all of your school's students felt the pride of building a school so another child could go to school. Well, you can! For a dollar.

ODFL will help your club or school organize a fundraiser where *every dollar donated goes into a developing world project*.

Make all of your school's students into heroes! It's easy, it's fun, and it's changing the world.

All profits from
The Best One Hour History™
series go to support ODFL.

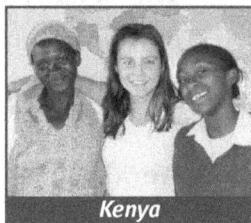

You see, you *can* change the world. *Now*, WILL you?

Visit: odfl.org

f OneDollar ForLife

email: info@odfl.org **Phone:** 661-203-8750

www.ingramcontent.com/pod-product-compliance
Lightning Source LLC
Chambersburg PA
CBHW060611030426
42337CB00018B/3036